To our [...] ught

To Lucinda B... 1977
Birthday Gift.

from

Fannie & Mildred
Whitead

Gisela Hein

Basic stitches
of embroidery

A modern approach

 VAN NOSTRAND REINHOLD COMPANY NEW YORK

Van Nostrand Reinhold Company Regional Offices:
New York Cincinnati Chicago Millbrae Dallas

German edition copyright © 1969 by Otto Maier Verlag, Ravensburg,
Germany

English translation copyright © 1971 by Litton Educational Publishing,
Inc.

Library of Congress Catalog Card Number: 79-118558

Published in the United States of America by
Van Nostrand Reinhold Company
450 West 33rd Street, New York, N.Y. 10001

16   15   14   13   12   11   10   9   8   7   6   5   4   3   2   1

Contents

Introduction

Fashion books have given us access to embroidery patterns dating from the time of the Renaissance and have provided a record of the changes in embroidery styles through the years. The superb collections of tapestries, embroidered clothing, and other articles in museums are further proof of the variety and complexity of artistic expression possible with needle and thread and bear witness to the widespread needlework skills and the understanding of color and form that existed centuries ago. This is evident in even the simplest ornamentations; the care taken with embroideries on even everyday utilitarian items of the past was clearly the result of great pleasure and satisfaction derived from individual creative expression in shapes, figures, and color.

Although embroidery is still practised today, there has been a gradual decline in its popularity. Modern industrial production has had an adverse effect on the interest in and the appreciation of the process of creative hand work; embroidery has become a factory technique, and for the most part the designs are of dubious merit. Recently, however, there has been a resurgence of interest in hand work, and embroidery is once more becoming a creative outlet for children and adults alike, as we shall see in the stitchery illustrated here.

In the wide range of embroidery stitches handed down to us we cannot always relate definite types to definite periods in time. A glance back over history reveals that at certain periods there seems to have been a preference for one or two types of stitches that determined both the style and creative quality of the work, and that in many areas (for example, in the monastries of the Middle Ages) this limitation led to the development of great artistic achievement in the craft. If we want to apply the value of such past experience to our own time, we should not demand technical perfection but instead we should nurture the ability to concentrate on a few technical and creative devices. This is particularly true in the case of embroidery for children.

The stitches and patterns described in this book were selected with care from the rich profusion available to us. They are a basis for accomplished work by adults and most of them can easily be done by children with very little instruction.

Embroidery

Success in embroidery is largely determined by the choice of materials and tools.
First of all, we need fabrics with a simple, regular weave, as for example, jute, hessian, linen, and certain woollen and cotton materials. A linen-type weave is distinguished by its simple crossed threads, produced by threading the weft through the warp. The warp threads are those stretched across the loom; the weft is the loose thread that is interwoven with the warp by means of a shuttle. A fabric takes on a totally different aspect after it has been embroidered.

The choice of embroidery threads obviously depends on the type of fabric; one must carefully balance the one with the other. Above all, the thickness of the thread needs to be taken into account; in only a few cases (such as needleweaving and appliqué) should the thread be coarser than the fabric itself. One must also bear in mind the different qualities of thread suitable for the type of work being planned.

On the whole, hemp threads, string, cotton, and woollen threads, as well as synthetic threads, are suitable. The chosen thread is worked through the fabric with an embroidery needle, which is distinguished from an ordinary sewing needle by its rounded point. The blunt point prevents catching and thus damaging and tearing the threads of the fabric. The size of the needle depends on the fineness of both fabric and embroidery thread (1). Prepared patterns should not be used in embroidery; the embroiderer herself should determine the size and thickness of stitches and how they are to be arranged, for only in this way will she be able to use the materials freely and discover her own standards in embroidery, thus attaining individual creative expression. The work can then be evaluated by her own personal criteria.

Sewing and Embroidery

Sewing has a technical function, embroidery a decorative one; yet there is a similarity in some respects. Normally, the stitches of a seam or hem are not visible, but a visible thread can often set off a seam, making it decorative as well as functional.

The running stitch on the hem (3) not only serves to attach the hem, but also to accentuate it. The same stitch is used in sewing as a tacking stitch (2).

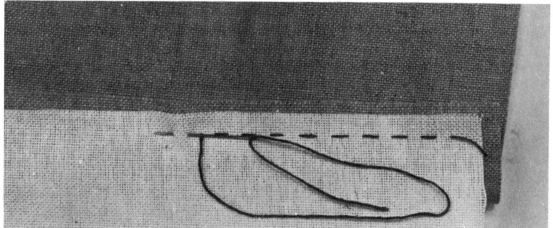

2

Decorative seams draw attention to the way the material is cut. However, they can also extend beyond the actual seam to cover a wider area of the material, a technique leading to embroidery for its own sake.

The weave of the fabric often serves as a guide, particularly in the case of coarsely woven materials such as linen. The contrast of fabric and thread is accentuated if the construction of the warp and weft is taken into account. The running stitch makes this particularly clear.

Close, even rows of running stitches form tiny geometrical shapes (3, 4, 5) whose sizes are determined by the rhythmical movement of the hand.

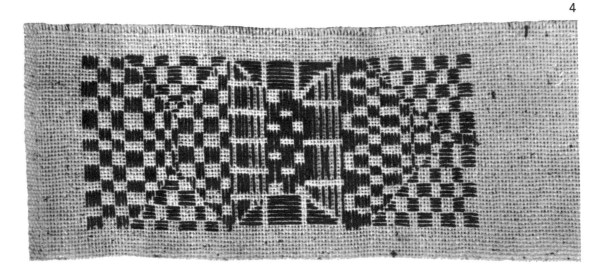

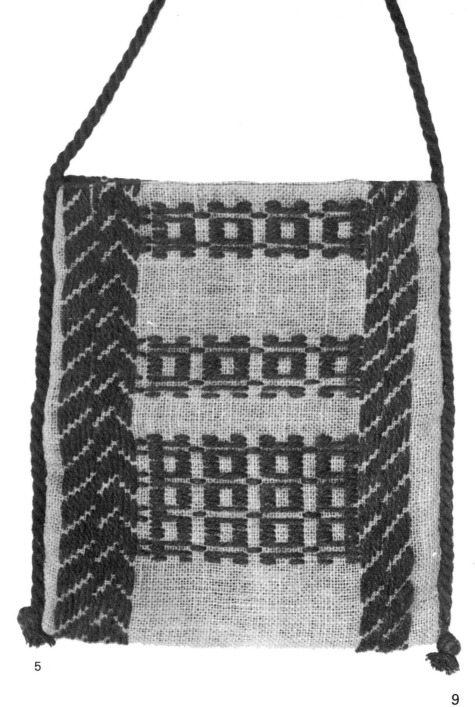

5

9

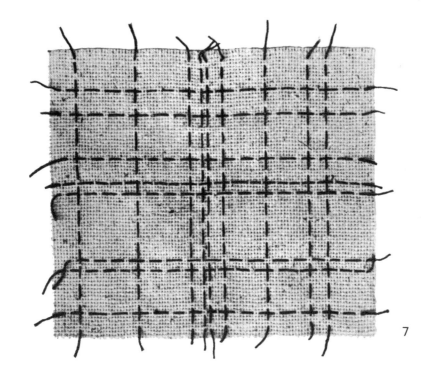

7

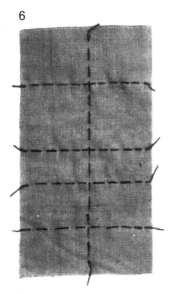

6

Close rows of stitches give a linear effect. Straight lines of running stitches that intersect each other divide the material into rectangles (6). The threads follow the weave of the material, thus repeating the same simple pattern. The uneven spacing between the rows of running stitches forms a rhythmical contrast to the coarse texture of the linen (7).

10

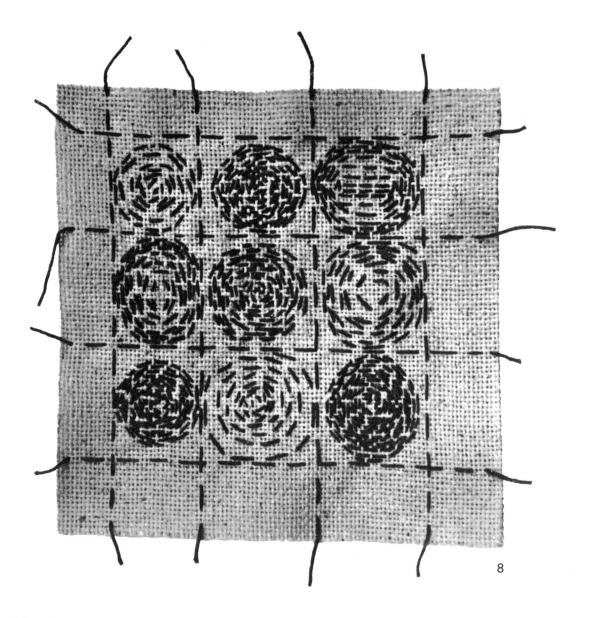

8

The large, open spaces of the rectangles demand to be filled in 8. Stitches forming circular patterns hide the weave of the material. The rectangles, following the weave of the material, bring the circles together to form a whole pattern.

9

Rhythmical Movement, as a natural means to well-known stitches.

Further reasons for different types of embroidery are apparent. Experience with ten-year-olds has led to the following observations: when a child embroiders, she does not worry about the normal rules of embroidery, but adopts the simple movement of slipping the needle in and out of the material. This spontaneous, rhythmical movement of the hand determines the kind of stitch produced; from these primary stitches one progresses to the well-known types of stitches. The running stitch is produced by a simple controlled movement of the arm (a). Many other stitches are created by a circular movement of the arm in a clockwise direction or, for a left-hander, in an anti-clockwise direction. The needle is slipped through the right side

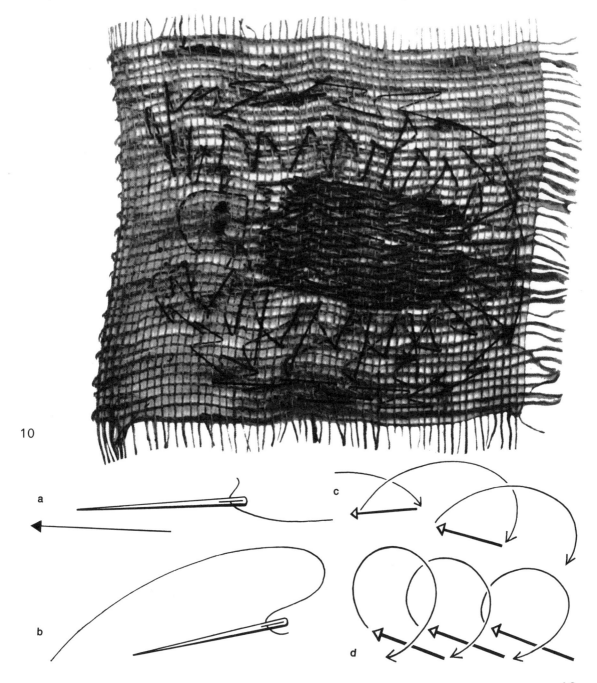

10

a

b

c

d

13

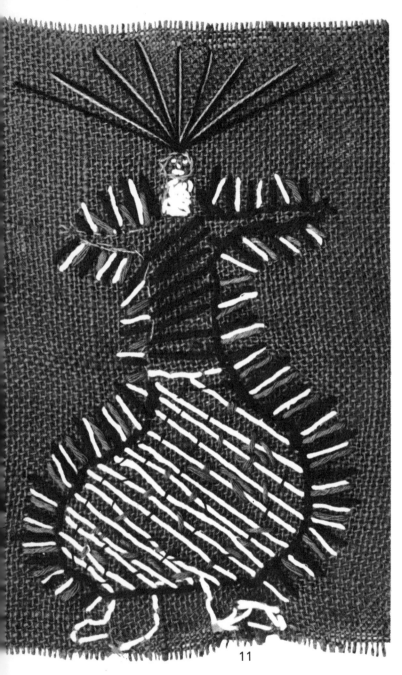

11

of the material and is pulled through from the wrong side leaving the required space between each stitch. The thread is pulled through in a wide circle, ready to form the next stitch (b, c, d). The stitch on the wrong side of the material is usually short, that is, no longer than the needle, and is measured by touch rather than sight. This is not the case with the right side of the material. Taking into account the stitches already there, the direction of the thread is determined by manipulation of both hand and arm. The pattern produced in embroidery rests entirely on the rhythmical mechanical movement and the tactile and visual processes involved.

Ten-year-old children with no previous experience in embroidery were able to embroider a centipede entirely unaided. One example (9) employs a stitch similar to the back stitch to form a sharp outline of the body. The back stitch is also used in sewing for stronger seams.

Jute is a loosely woven fabric, and consequently in embroidery the stitches on the wrong side of the material show through (10).

The formation of different types of stitches should be noted in illustration 11: the herringbone stitch, satin stitch, couching and stem stitch.

Long, flat stitches fill the bottle-shaped body. Longer threads are sewn down by short couching stitches. Contours, color contrasts, and a rhythmical arrangement of stitches are the main features of this individualistic piece of embroidery.

Types of Stitches,

developed from a rhythmical movement

1 Stem stitch and back stitch
2 Satin stitch
3 Chained stitches (chain and button-hole stitch)
4 Herringbone stitch
5 Long filling stitch

The manipulation of the arm, the way the needle is held, and the direction of the stitch are all crucial to the following types of stitches: parallel, interwoven, and crossed stitches which are developed independently. One stitch does not necessarily follow from another, but rather the pattern determines the choice of stitch. The chosen stitches should naturally form an aesthetically pleasing and technically coherent pattern.

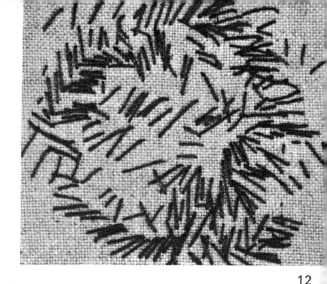

12

If we do not control the manipulation of the arm, we are not able to keep the stitches in a straight line, and so simply produce a maze of uneven stitches (12). Even rows of stitches demand both optical control and a steady movement of the arm and hand, which becomes tiring after a while particularly for children. This mechanical action can be varied and made more stimulating if the direction of the stitch and thus the position of the needle is changed after each row (13).

13

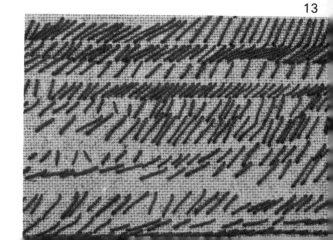

14

1 Stem stitch and back stitch

The easiest method of embroidery is with the needle held roughly parallel to the body pointed right-to-left. Simple straight stitches are then produced such as the stem stitch and back stitch (see also 13). The stem stitch is worked from left to right (a). The needle is slipped through the material and is pulled through. From the wrong side, halfway up the previous stitch and just to the side of it, the needle is inserted and pulled through ready to start the next stitch.

The back stitch is worked from the right (b). For each stitch the thread is worked to the right to the length of one stitch; on the wrong side of the material the thread takes the length of two stitches forwards, that is to the left.

a   Stem stitch

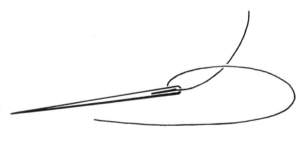

b   Back stitch

16

Both stitches are suitable for line patterns. The stem stitch can form loops and curves (14), and has a bolder effect than back stitch (15), which is worked in a straight, even line. For curves the stitch has to be shortened. The slant illustrated in the stem stitch is determined by the position of the hand. As the row becomes steeper, the hand must turn, until it becomes so difficult to manipulate that we have to turn the material to its natural position again. Here the rows form vertical lines, rather like a page of Chinese writing.

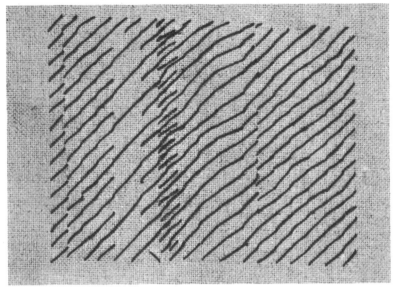

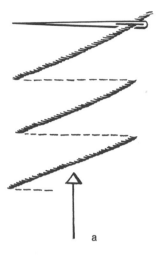

16

17

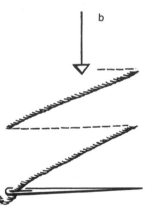

18

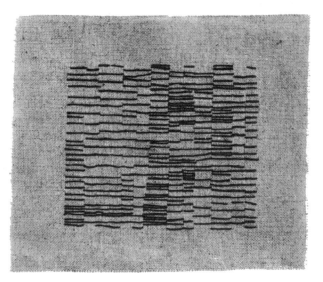

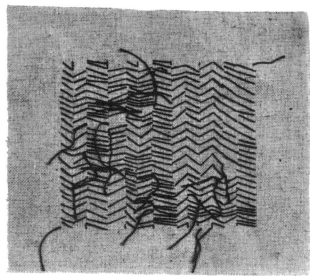

18

19

Bearing the previous directions in mind, we work the rows from top to bottom and vice versa. The illustrations clearly show how the pattern depends both on the direction of the stitches and the position of the needle (a, b). The embroidery in 16 is the product of (a). After each row the material was turned around in order to start the next row. In 17 the rows are worked in various directions, some meeting and crossing each other. Here the material is also turned when necessary.

The working of the material and the end product cannot be fully grasped until one has seen the formation of stitches on the wrong side of the material. Here one sees how the pattern has taken shape (18, 19).

2 Satin stitch

The closer the stitches lie together on the right side, the closer the resemblance between the pattern formed on each side of the material. If the stitches are worked very closely together, they cover the entire surface of the material. This type of stitch is called satin stitch. It is particularly suitable as a filling-in stitch.

20

21

The shoulder bands (20, 21) are filled in completely. Here the satin stitch has created an entirely new surface of colored shapes by using a soft woollen thread.

In addition to this stitch we must also mention the 'slanted satin stitch', which is worked from left to right (a). Care should be taken to keep the needle under the thread. If it is caught in the thread, loops will be formed (b). This is a basis for further types of stitches, simple examples being the buttonhole stitch, feather stitch, and chain stitch.

3 Chained stitches

For the buttonhole stitch, the needle is generally held vertically, with the point facing downwards. The thread is looped beneath the point of the needle before pulling it through (c). One stitch is thus linked with another. The buttonhole stitch is invaluable for covering raw edges; the loops prevent the material from fraying, hence the need to hold the needle vertically.

We can give the stitch a rounded V-shape by inserting the needle at a slant. We begin each stitch inside the V-angle (d), thus forming a diagonal pattern. If we keep changing the direction of the needle we get an alternating row of stitches (e), generally called feather stitch. In 22 the feather stitch has been worked over the entire surface to form a net-like pattern.

For chain stitch the needle is always put in the link at the point at which it last came out (f). This can be used both for rows and for covering large surfaces of material.

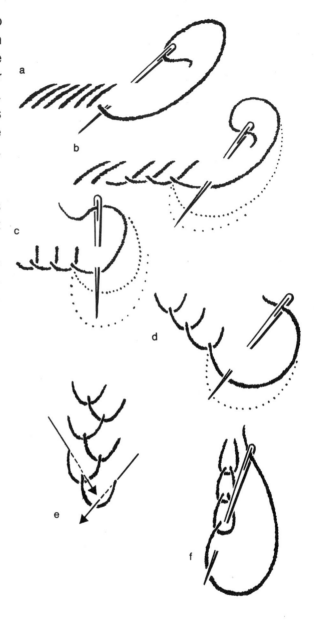

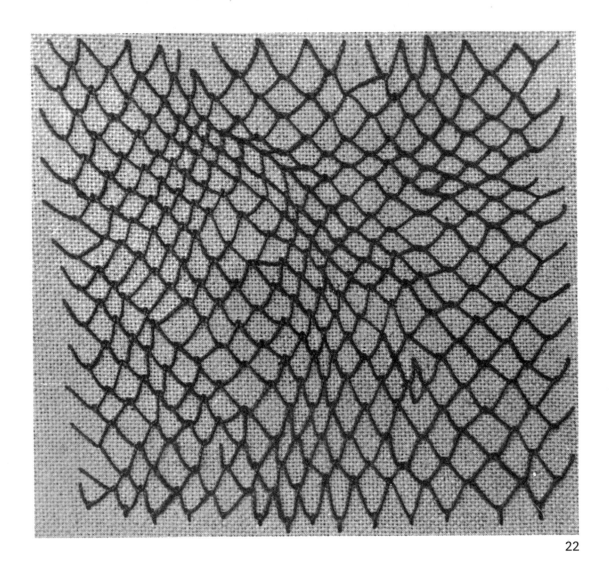

22

Herringbone stitch

a

b

22

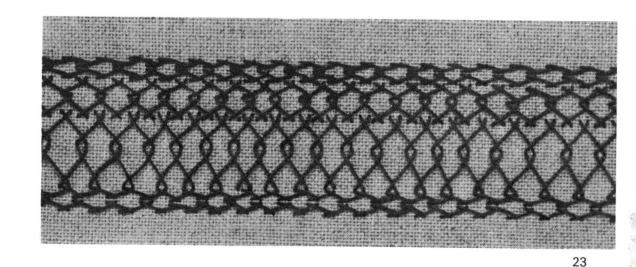

4 Herringbone stitch

The herringbone stitch is a variation of the stem stitch. The needle is inserted and pulled through the material to form a straight line (a). Each time the thread is pulled through, however, it is placed to the side of the previous stitch, thus causing overlapping (24). If we depart from the straight line by starting every other stitch slightly lower down, we get the herringbone stitch (b). This stitch can lead to many variations (23, 25).

24

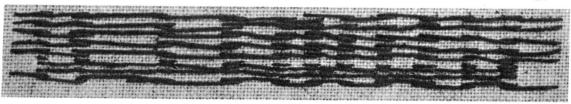

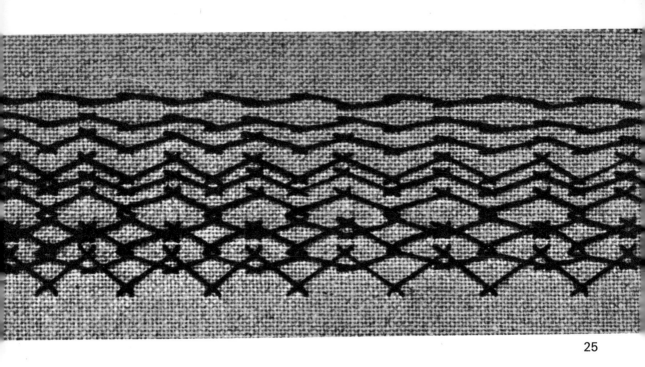

The herringbone stitch is very flexible. This becomes clear if we disregard the weave of the material (26). Here the stitches are very long and overlap each other; some of the stitches are so long that they require a short stitch to secure the thread to the material.

A long stitch secured at the centre by a short stitch is shown in (a). For this, the needle is returned to the center of the long stitch to make a short catch stitch.

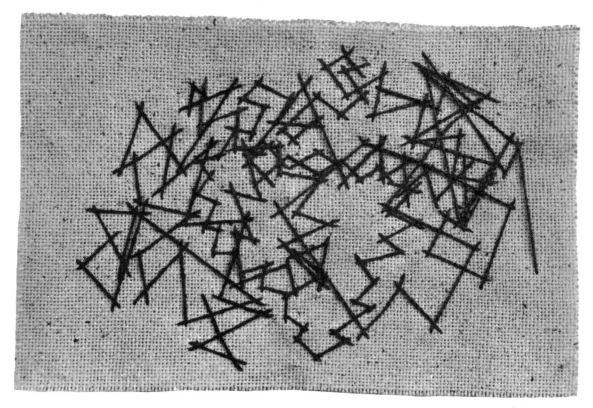

26

Catch stitch

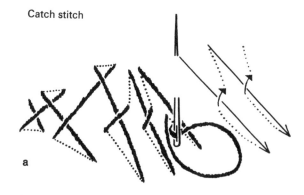

a

25

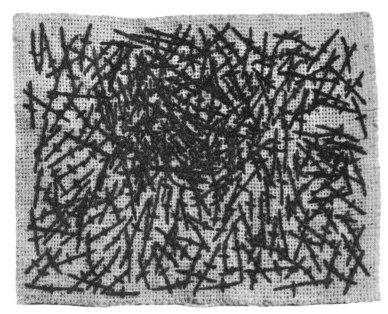

27

28

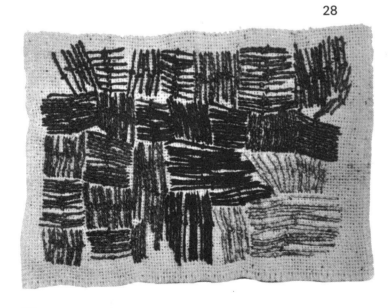

26

29

5 Long filling stitch

A dense 'maze' of stitches gives the material a completely new texture (27). This stitch is ideal for filling in large surfaces, as in 28.

The long, open, filling stitch is ideal for tapestry work. Long stitches, secured by short couching stitches can cover any surface, regardless of size. In 29 the couching stitches form rows of knots, securing the loosely worked filling stitches.

Types of Stitches, developed as a contrast to the weave

1 Simple cross stitch (petit point and gros point)
2 Alternating cross stitch

Cross stitch has been developed as a contrast to the horizontal and vertical weave of a fabric. It is not, therefore, produced by a rhythmical movement, but on the contrary is one of the few stitches bound by the weave of the material. Cross stitch is always worked diagonally across the warp and weft threads, over a square or rectangle.

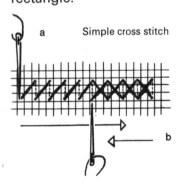

a Simple cross stitch

b

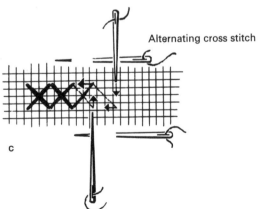

Alternating cross stitch

c

The two kinds of cross stitch differ in their structural formation:

1 Simple cross stitch begins as petit point (that is, the single, diagonal tent stitch) and is completed with a crossed diagonal stitch to form a gros point or cross stitch (a, b). It is the ideal stitch for filling-in work (31, 32), for decorative work and for letter embroidery (30).

2 Alternating cross stitch is worked by changing the direction of the needle each time the thread is pulled through the material (c). In this way the stitches vary in the way they cross over each other, thus relieving the uniformity of the simple cross stitch.

For cross stitch one needs a strong, lattice-like material, a coarse linen, sieve linen, or canvas (31, 32), for the full effect of the stitch is achieved entirely by the contrast between the cross stitch and the weave of the material.

31

32

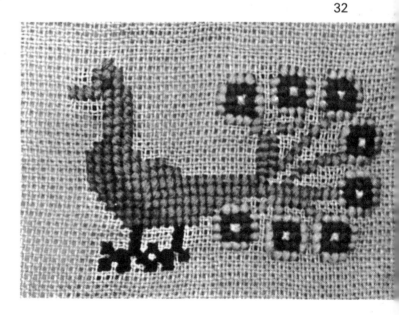

33   34   35

Close-set cross stitches can cover large areas and even the entire surface of the material. Rows of larger, open cross stitches form a lattice; the spaces thus produced form a contrasting background (33, 34, 35).

Embroidery is usually a repetitive process, which can often lead to a merely mechanical row formation, particularly with the cross stitch. It becomes more stimulating if we break away from the repetitive row formation and occasionally introduce the alternating cross stitch. Stitches of different width but of the same length joined together both vertically and horizontally can form a 'maze' (36).

On this napkin or handkerchief case (37) rows of cross stitches are made to form a symmetrical pattern. The gradual increase and decrease in the width of the stitch produces the light-dark contrast.

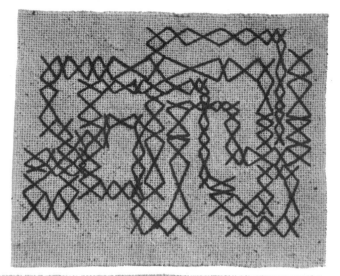

36

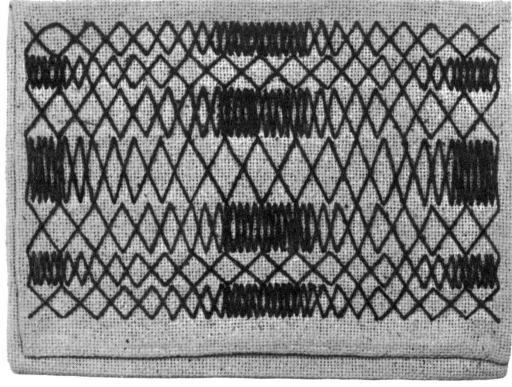

37

38

39

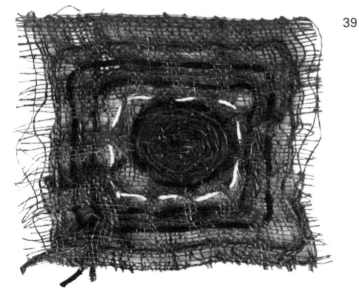

32

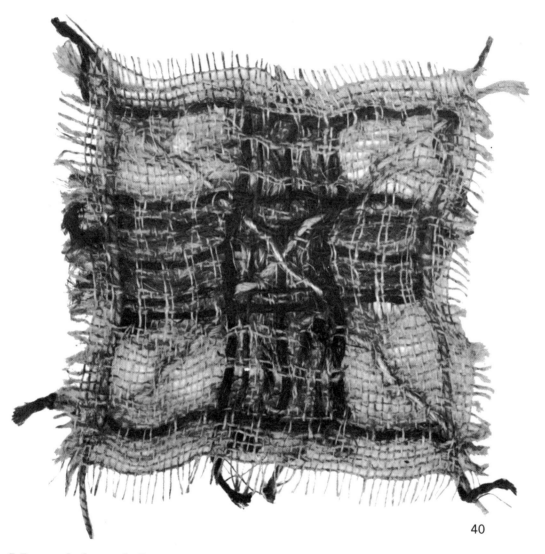

40

Material and Structure

Coarse fabrics and thick, strong threads give an understanding of the limits set by the material, and yet provide great scope for the imagination. They can be embroidered without a needle, thereby giving children an opportunity to 'physically' grasp the process of embroidery. Children react naturally and spontaneously.

'Early forms of child-like figures' are revived in the work produced by ten-year-olds, evidence of creative skills worth preserving and developing (38, 39, 40). They make clear the fact that these pieces of embroidery should not be judged by adult standards but by the child's stage of development.

Jute and hessian are simple, coarse fabrics; together with multi-thread fabrics such as hemp and sisal, they are ideal for learning about materials. Coarse threads are not suitable for small patterns; the simplest method is to pull them through the material in one direction (38). In 39 the tautly twisted thread produces a snail-like effect. The center is enhanced by an oval spiral that fits neatly into the rectangle. In 40, diagonals form a link between the wide cross and the corners of the pattern. The basic areas of the rectangle are thus outlined. The patterns in 38, 39, and 40 were each worked without a needle; instead the ends of the threads were dipped in liquid wax or were simply bent over. The actual process of pulling thread in and out through material was thus experienced more forcibly. Children enjoy working out their own color schemes, as was the case in the examples shown here. By using a needle and finer thread more intricate patterns can be produced. Variations of the basic pattern are seen in the crosses and stars (41, 42, 43).

41   42

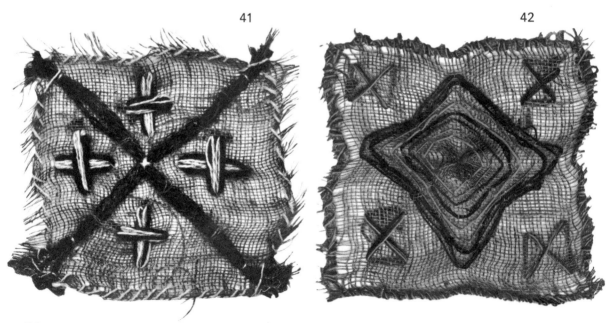

43

44

45

46

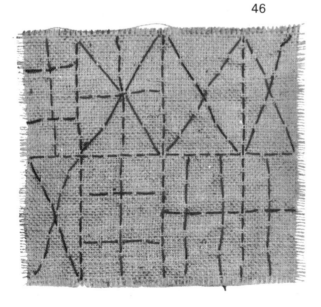

Simple straight lines divide the material into rectangles, which then call for further decoration. In 46 the rectangles enclose diagonals and crosses; the restriction has thus led to a simple, uniform pattern. The four rectangles in 45 also brought pleasing results; the rectangles correspond diagonally, and the larger diagonals are repeated in the pattern. With nine rectangles (44), the center one is enhanced. These three examples are typical of the imaginative work of ten-year-olds.

47

48

Such creativity can be encouraged and advanced only if there is no model or pattern to follow, which is the case in all the work illustrated in this book.

If the material itself is already patterned, the texture no longer provides the main stimulus; squares and stripes in the fabric, for example, can form a basis for embroidery (47, 48).

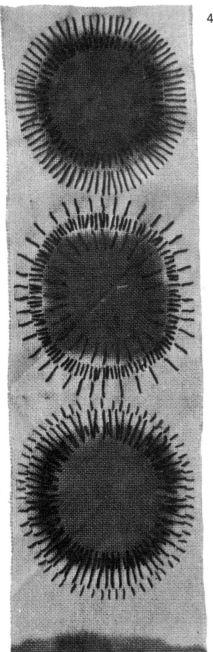

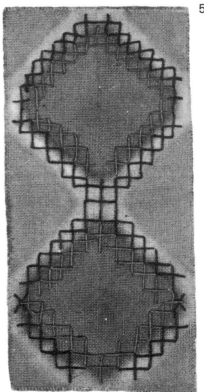

The Application of Stitches on Self-dyed Materials

Self-dyed materials can provide a stimulating basis for embroidery. The main object is to find or make up suitable stitches, and to work them into the pattern. After careful planning and consideration the dyed patterns can be set off, completely isolated, or connected by the embroidery thread. The thread thus lends the finishing touch.

In the so-called 'dip-dye' process, the outlines of the dyed patterns are usually blurred. Shapes

are simple: circles, rectangles, triangles. They gain effect through the color contrast, and we can use them effectively as a basis for our embroidery pattern. By dye-dipping the center and edges of a cloth that has been folded twice we get a bright circle. The circle is worked with a dark herringbone stitch (51), thus decreasing its intense brightness.

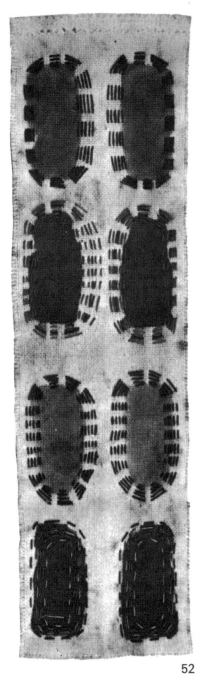

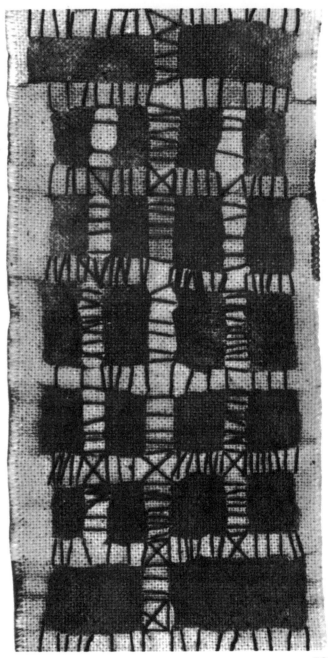

52

53

40

54

The oval shapes (52) were dipped and dyed in wax. The running stitches worked around the shapes harmonise with the white background and the color patterns.
In 53 and 54 a candle was used as a resist, the dye being dripped onto the material. The thread helps to balance the contrasting colors.

Embroidery is not suitable for every batik fabric. One must decide whether the pattern is already complete or whether it suggests further decoration. In 55 and 56 the lines of wax resist are finished off and certain shapes enhanced.

55

56

57

58

Embroidery stitches provide the finishing touches to the wax-dyed figures (57, 58).

59

60

Weaving and Embroidery

Weaving also provides a basis for the formation of embroidery patterns. There is an obvious connection between the Cretan embroidery (wrong side of band), and the weaving pattern. This was quite

61

common in early creative art. In 59 the wefts combine to form a pattern. In 60 the satin stitch is worked by holding the needle and thread parallel to the weave of the material. In 61 and 62 regular shortening of the stitches produced the diagonal pattern characteristic of the weaving technique.

62

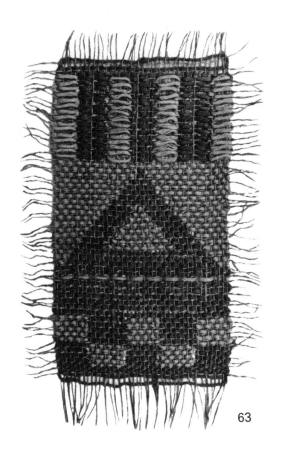

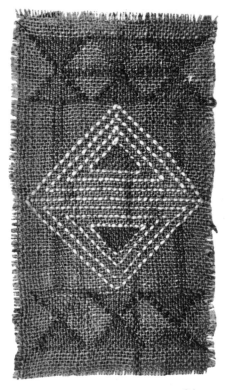

63   64

Knowledge of the different weave structures helps one understand how to embellish the weave with embroidery stitches. In loose jute the weave can itself be added to by pulling through additional threads (63). In 64 hessian running stitch was worked diagonally across the threads of the material. This simple kind of embroidery is suitable for group work. On a large piece of jute, 28⊥44 inches, various patterns are combined to form a contrast (65). The group found a common basis in the relationship between the texture of the material, the diamond shapes, and the colors (red and green).

46

65

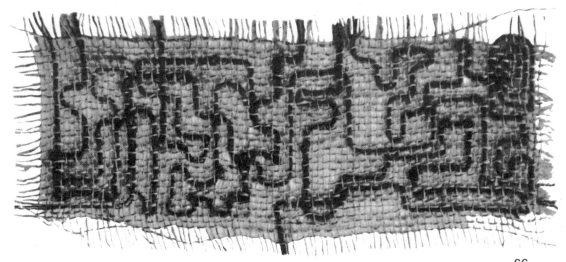

Changing the Structure of the Weave

1 Needleweaving
2 Smock technique, Stretch stitch embroidery, Open embroidery
3 Hemstitch
We can change the structure of the weave by interweaving threads of various types and strengths, by pulling thread taut, and by pulling out warp or weft threads. Each of these processes is complete in itself.

1 Needleweaving
Threads are interwoven with the warp and weft, both horizontally and vertically, forming curves and straight lines (66).
Interweaving is especially effective on tulle: circles and loops can be worked around the large, open stitches (69).

67

68 →

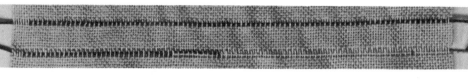

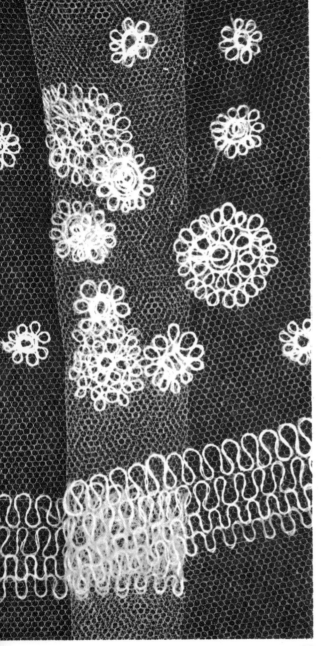

For coarse weaves the needle-weaving technique is ideal. Two or more weft or warp threads are replaced by a new thread. The new thread is first knotted to the warp or weft thread and pulled through with it (67). Very coarse threads completely change the appearance of the material (71); in order to pull them through either a tapestry needle must be used (70) or the ends dipped in wax.

A section of a bag (68) shows a combination of running stitch and needle weaving. The colored sisal threads lend the dull sack cloth a bright appearance and enrich the coarse texture of the material.

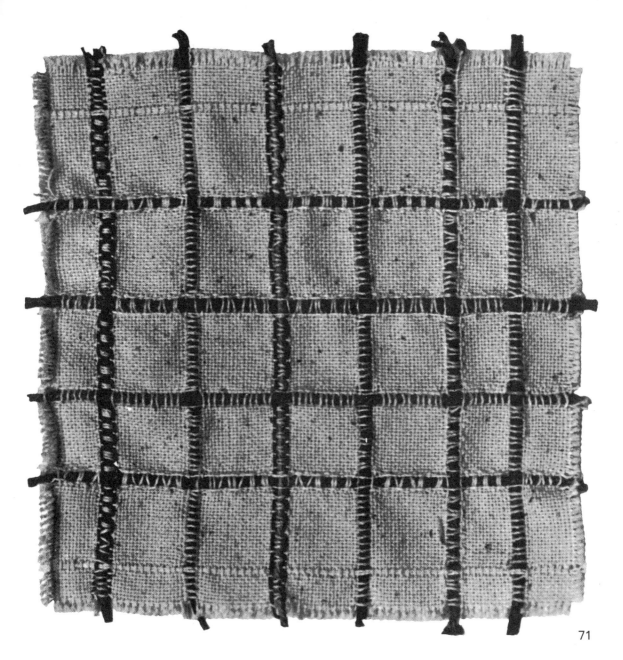

Short, close-set running stitches form gathers (72) if the thread is pulled taut. This process is called 'gathering'. If gathering stitches are sewn in evenly spaced rows, the material falls into folds (73a). The folds can be made to form patterns and held in place by catch stitches (73b).

2 Smock technique

The smock technique also involves the process of gathering. The gathering threads serve as guiding threads and are pulled out after the smocking is completed. The actual smocking stitch (catch stitch) arranges the material into pleats, to form the characteristic honeycomb pattern (74a, 74b, 75) The catch stitch is looped around each pair of folds twice in the same place. It can remain visible on the surface or hidden under the fold. To produce a ruffled effect, two-and-a-half to three times the normal amount of material is required.

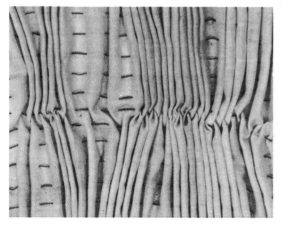

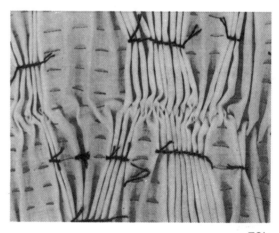

73a

73b

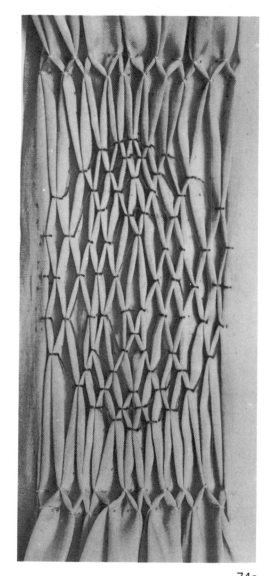

74a

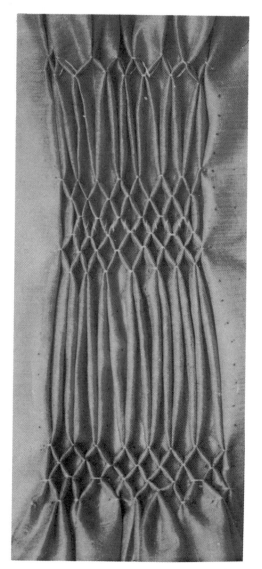

74b

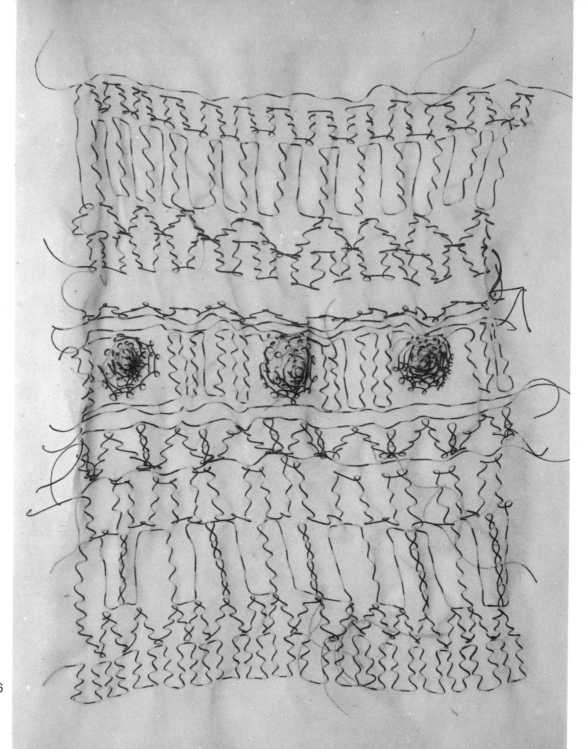

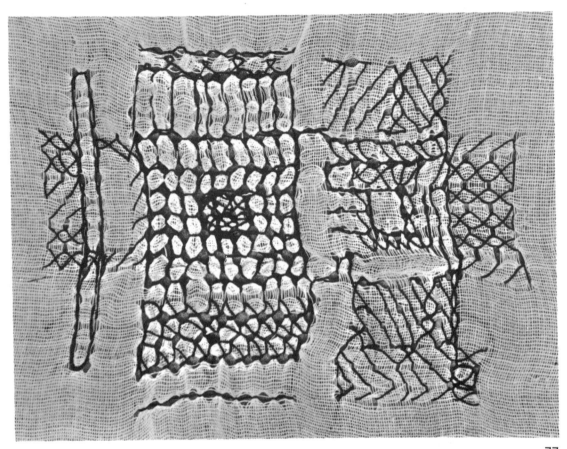

Stretch stitch embroidery

A thread pulled tautly through the material stays firm and creates a wavy effect. Fine material, such as georgette, gives a particularly charming ruffled effect (76). In a loose weave, threads are forced from their original position. If we bind these threads together, open spaces appear (77). Thus one can alter the texture of a fabric by binding its threads together (78, 79). For this technique sieve linen is generally used.

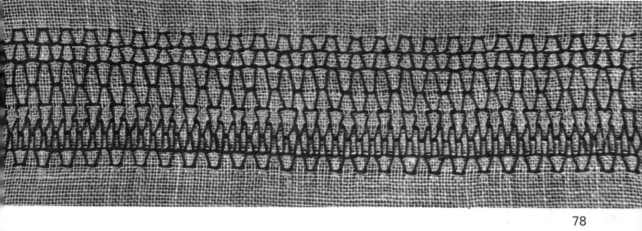

78

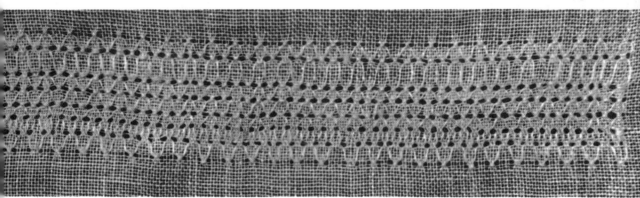

79

Open Embroidery

To make the holes in the fabric even larger, one stitches around the holes, forcing the surrounding threads as far apart as possible, and binding them to the neighbouring threads. This technique is particularly suited for the mask (80). Compared with jute, the tautly woven sieve linen leaves only small holes (81). For larger circles in sieve linen one cuts the diameters to the desired length, turns the edges and stitches around them to form a circle (82).

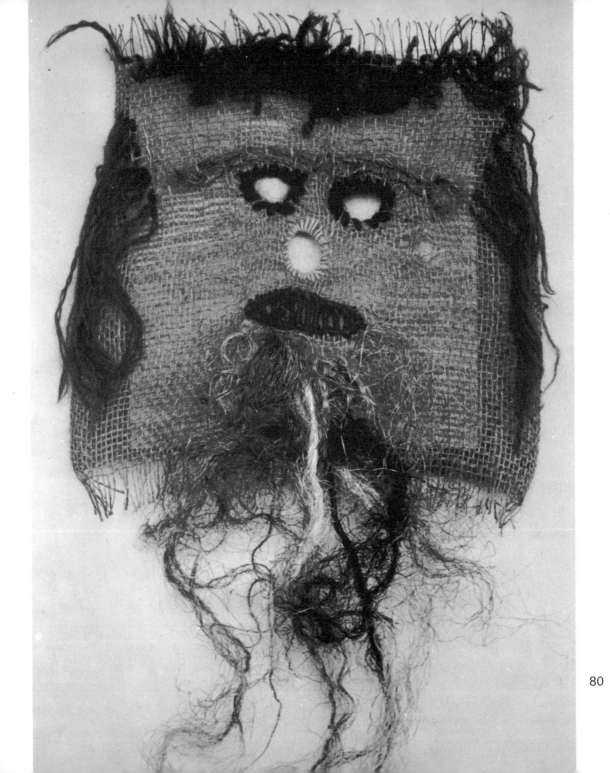

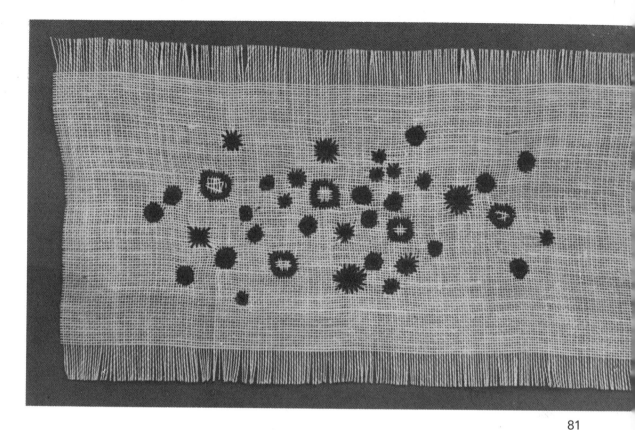

81

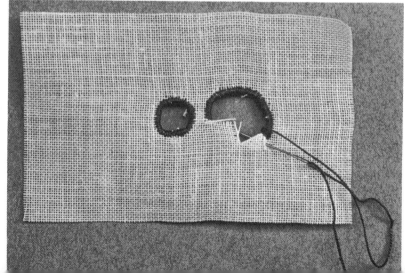

82

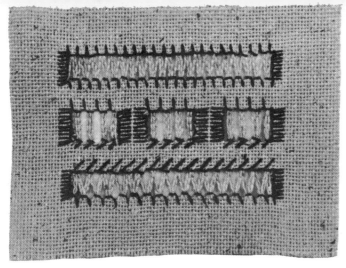

83

3 Hem stitch

For this stitch threads are pulled out, in one direction, from certain planned sections of the fabric, leaving single threads. This 'exposed' section forms the basis for the work. Hem stitching strengthens the edges by binding the remaining threads and fastening the raw edges of the material at top and bottom (a, b). The raw edges at the sides are simply strengthened with buttonhole stitch (83).

Hem stitch is frequently used for table-cloths and napkins, etc. The stitch strengthens the hem, thus giving the essential hemming process a decorative function.

The hem stitch can also produce a filigree-type pattern (84). Here herringbone stitch is looped around the warp and weft threads. It is the ideal stitch for close-set open sections of material.

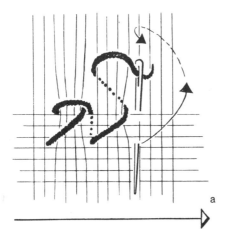

a

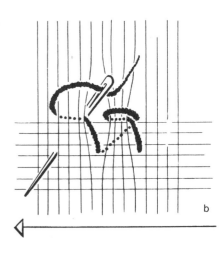

b

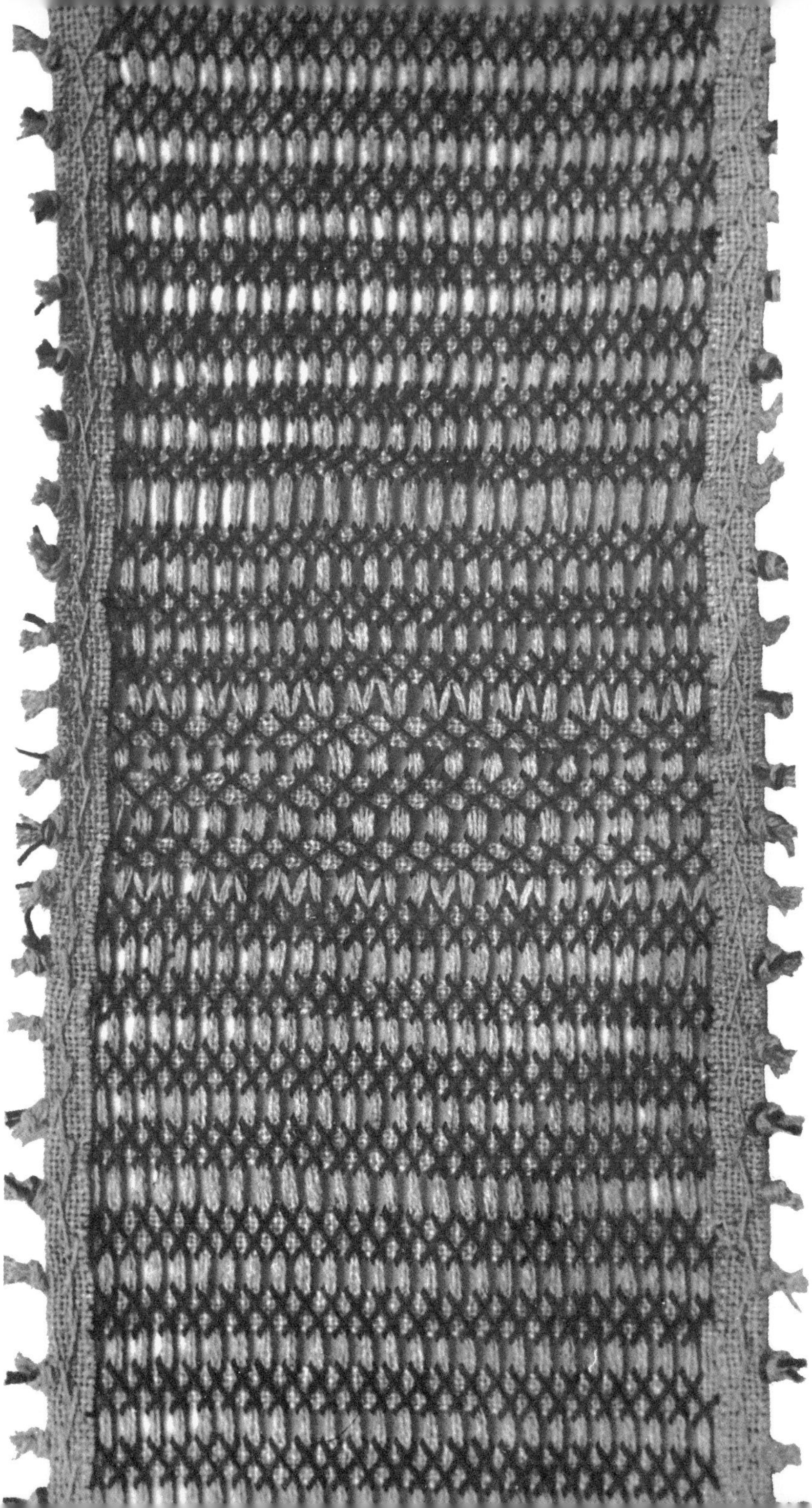

85

Hem stitch was used on this lined bag (85) to join the two pieces together, but it also has a decorative function. The loose threads in the middle panel are tied in the center. Here hem stitch is unnecessary because both warp and weft threads are held together securely. The lining thus makes the bag serviceable.

86 87

Appliqué, an extension of embroidery

Some decorative stitches also have a practical function: the blanket stitch (page 21, c) binds the raw edge of the material; smock stitch (75) gathers and shapes articles of clothing; hem stitch (page 60, a, b) binds hems; it can also join two loose pieces of material together (85).

The decorative stitch thus has a practical function in sewing. A wide field of application is the method known by the French term appliqué, whereby pieces of material are sewn onto a background material. It is a technique involving a great deal of creative imagination (86, 87). A simple form of appliqué is seen in the 'chessboard' pattern (88). The squares are applied with diagonal stitches. By overcasting the edges we protect them from fraying (89). Edges of simple shapes can be turned under and hemmed. With the 'Theatre Man' (86) the edges of the material are covered with seam-binding and stitched down with tiny running stitches. Hair, eyes, mouth, and buttons are also fastening stitches. The two thematically similar pieces of work 86 and 87 reveal different modes of expression. The pleasure found in gathering and pleating, that is the ability to *form*, is common to both of them.

Thread Appliqué

Applying threads to the material by means of a second thread or by knotting is also a feature of appliqué. Illustrations 90 and 91 show cylindrical animal shapes covered with jute, embroidered, and draped with threads, thus giving the animals a coat of fur.

91

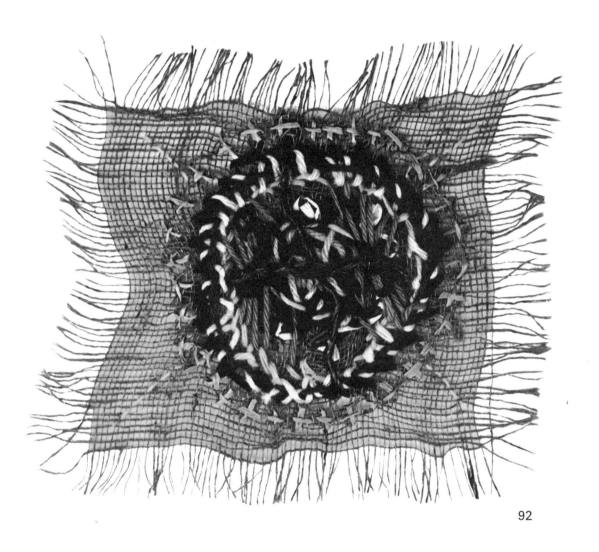

92

Knots of wool, held in place by overcasting, are embedded in a 'nest' (92).
A tautly twisted thread is extremely elastic. This can be seen in 93, where coarse
string is arranged in curves and spirals. In the center the strings are twisted to form
contrasting circles. This is an example of the vast possibilities open to the creative
mind in the arrangement of threads into attractive patterns.

67

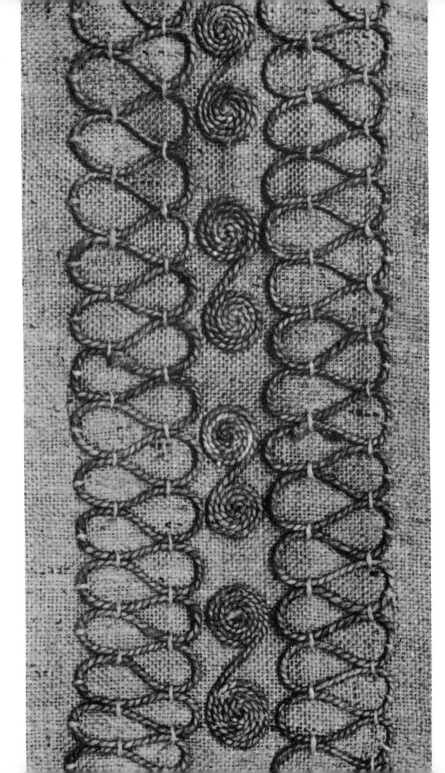

93

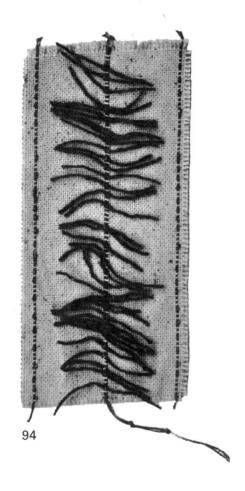

94

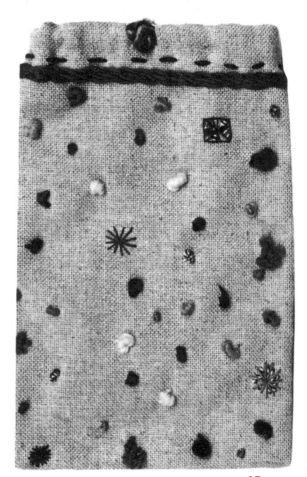

95

a

The short woollen fringe of the book-marker (94) is attached by a single thread. The coloured knots on the linen bag (95) are an example of the knot stitch (a), which gives a bead effect.

In addition to the thread and the material, beads, felt, leather, baste, and other natural fibers are all suitable for appliqué work.

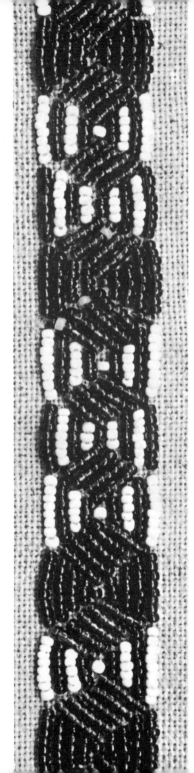

Bead Embroidery

Beads are a very attractive medium for children. The spherical shapes appeal to their sense of touch, the shine of the colored glass gives immense pleasure. The first step in this technique is to dot beads here and there in an arbitrary fashion as in 97. In this way children learn to make use of single beads. The arrangement of beads to cover a whole surface is then only a second step. Since several beads may be held on one stitch,

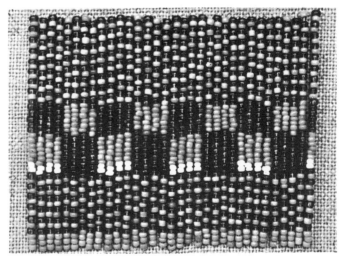

very compact rows can be formed relatively quickly.

The color contrast on the band of beads (96) shows that each stitch holds up to eight beads. They are relatively short strings and can be arranged in any order independent of the weave formation. Threading different colored beads on longer threads produces rich patterns; lively patterns appear by repeating and changing parallel strings, alternating and mixing groups of colors (98).

Chains arranged in spirals are attached to the material by stitching with a separate thread (99). Here we have adopted both the technical and creative aspect of threading. In 100 the square wooden beads need to be arranged in strict sequence. Here they are worked in between the threads of jute, to form a level surface.

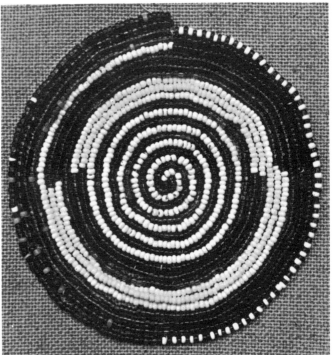

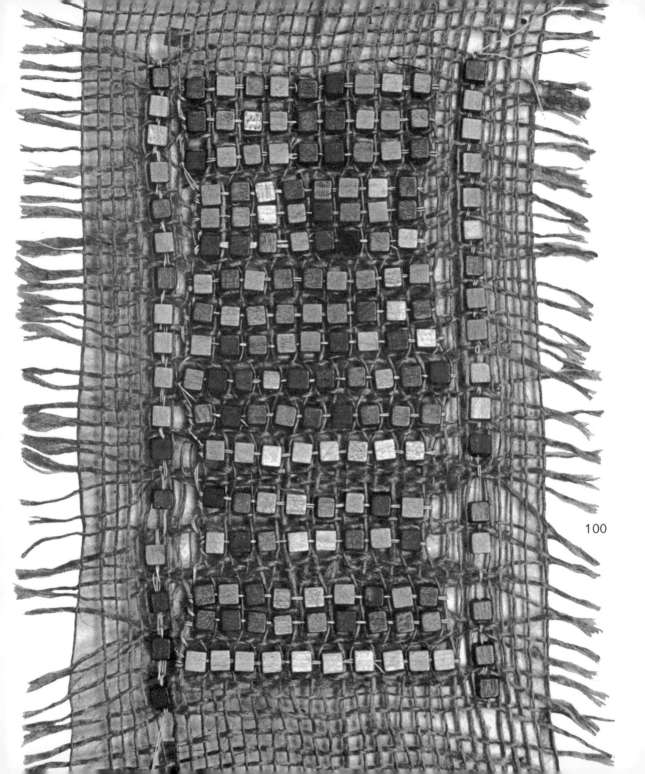

100

101

Color Effects in Embroidery

Colored threads not only change the structure of the material, but also affect the tone of the color. Color effects such as blending and contrast should always be taken into account in embroidery. It is best to limit oneself to just a few colors.

If we dye our own embroidery thread, we can choose and blend colors to our own liking. Dyeing one's own material and thread is a rewarding task involving creative thought and imagination, and can often bring unexpected and pleasing results.

With the tie-and-dye process we can resist sections of the yarn (103) thus producing alternating patterns of color. The bright color effect is enhanced by the plain background (102). The even regularity of the pattern is emphasised by the uniformity in length of the stitches. The running stitch is ideal for this purpose.

102

103

Embroidery with the Sewing Machine

Needlework formerly comprised only handwork. Today the sewing machine (104) has also been used for embroidery. 'Stitch tests' (105) show a graphic effect. The technique of machine embroidery somewhat resembles a drawing technique; one does not determine the individual stitch during the course of the work, but rather the length of the lines of stitches and their direction. Careful attention to holding and guiding the material and starting and stopping the machine is the basis for establishing a sense of rhythm. The following embroidery can be done with the sewing machine. The quilting seam is already familiar to us. It can be used for single rows or for covering entire surfaces.

With the so-called zig-zag adaptation the needle jumps from side to side; this is different from the quilting seam in that we not only set the length of the stitch, but also its span or width. Both can be changed during the course of the work.

A longer, narrower stitch gives the line a wavy appearance. The result is particularly vivid if the lines are longer (107). If the stitches are wider than

104

105

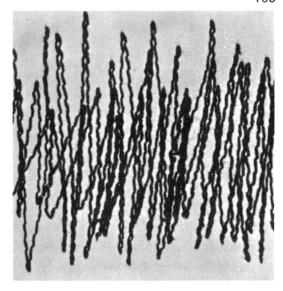

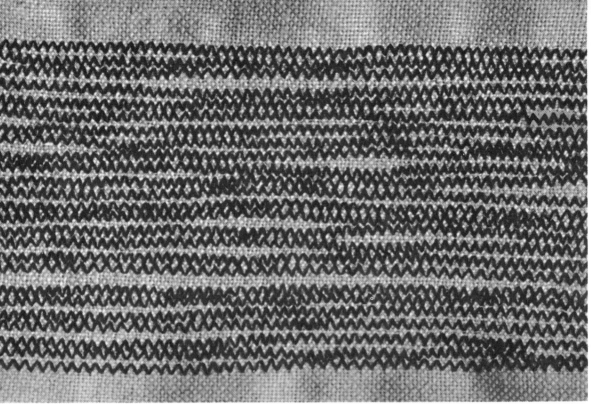

the length they form a kind of satin stitch (108).

If the length and width are equal the result is the marked zig-zag stitch. We get a slightly wavy effect if we do not keep to a straight line; by setting the rows apart the spaces form a bright contrast (106).

For fine materials the work is stretched onto an embroidery frame, in order to avoid puckering.

With machine embroidery one can produce long lines relatively quickly and easily. Difficulties arise, particularly for the beginner, if the rows are short and worked in several directions. For appliqué work (109), in which the edges are applied by minute stitches, previous experience with machine sewing is essential.

Length and width of a stitch are set before commencing work, according to the strength and thickness of the material. Since, however, material shows a rhythmical structure in the weave formation, the mechanical machine stitch can never quite adjust to it. The line of stitching, therefore, need not necessarily follow the weave of the material (107).

Double thread can be used on the machine, forming similar stitches on each side of the material. One can thus use either side of the material. The 'wrong' side of the material is distinguishable if we use threads of different colors. If, during the course of the work, we turn the material over and consider the wrong side as the right side, the two colors will appear on both sides. The types of stitches described here are developed from the quilting seam and are subject to the uniformity of stitches produced by the machine. One can also adapt the machine to certain types of stitches usually performed by hand such as the hemstitch. Yet even here one is bound to the regularity of machine stitches; this is the essential difference between machine embroidery and hand embroidery.

For machine embroidery one should not only have practical experience but also a knowledge of creative effects and the types of material used. Handwork will give us this necessary insight and knowledge. Hand embroidery provides an inexhaustible source for creative expression.